HOW TO
PROCRASTINATE

THE *Self-Hurt* SERIES

**KNOCK
KNOCK**
VENICE, CALIFORNIA

Published by
Knock Knock
1633 Electric Avenue
Venice, CA 90291
www.knockknock.biz

Illustrated by Mark Weber

ISBN: 978-160106043-3
UPC: 8-25703-50105-6

CONTENTS

CHAPTER 1
INTRODUCTION:
EXPAND TIME WITH PROCRASTINATION

WE LIVE IN AN OVERBOOKED AND hurried world ruled by schedules, goals, and ever-lengthening to-do lists. The more efficient we get, the more work we take on. The pressures and demands are enough to send us running back to our prehistoric caves in order to free ourselves from the imperatives of electricity, motors, and upward mobility. If you're reading this book, you haven't yet found a reasonable way to extricate yourself from the rat race. The solution, however, has been with you all along, and with a little bit of work, you'll be able to loosen the noose. What's this miracle cure to modern malaise? A time-lending tool called procrastination.

Procrastination is the art of finding time for yourself by delaying action on a project or task. You can dedicate these "stolen" hours to doing other, more fun things or (ideally) to doing nothing at all. Most people suffer under the delusion that procrastination is an inborn skill, but procrastination can be learned by even the most efficient, productive workaholics. "How do you get to Carnegie Hall?" a tourist needing directions asks. "Practice, practice, practice," replies the old joke. It's the same with procrastination: if you put in the effort, you'll get there . . . tomorrow (and that's the procrastinator's metaphoric tomorrow, not the day after today).

By picking up this book, you're already a few steps ahead of the rat-race rabble, and we're going to help you embrace the procrastinator you've always wanted to be.

Not only will you develop the tools to procrastinate, you'll increase your motivation to stall, no matter how much of a go-getter you are now. Your transformation will include such lessons as:

- Why procrastination is such a personally rewarding way to work and live.

- What type of efficiency maven or achiever you are, and how to overcome those negative behavior patterns.

- How to harness time to work for you rather than the other way around.

- How to create the right environment *not* to work.

- What to do while procrastinating at home or at the office.

- How to assess whether you should do work or just . . . do nothing.

Deferred Words

"Procrastination isn't the problem, it's the solution.
So procrastinate now—don't put it off."
—Ellen DeGeneres

Why Procrastinate?

Why *not* procrastinate? There are more
reasons to procrastinate than there are to
get something done. In fact, if you weren't
aspiring to be a procrastinator, you could
spend some time writing them all down.
But this book is here to make it easier for
you, so it's all spelled out below.

Self-Knowledge Cultivation

When you spend the majority of your
time working toward the expectations
and deadlines of others, it's all too
common to lose sight of what's most

important—you. You'll spend the time you save through work postponement on daydreaming, fantasizing about the future, revisiting old hobbies, discovering hidden talents, pulling the lint out of your bellybutton, and exploring anything and everything that interests you.

You Deserve a Break

Come on—don't you? Isn't there more to life than work? When do *you* get *your* turn? It's not tomorrow, not next week, not next month—it's now! By properly and deliberately delaying your duties and shirking your responsibilities, the resulting mental break will not only be enjoyable, it'll clear your mind to perform better when it's finally time to buckle down.

More Time with Friends

When was the last time you had a simple, unplanned chat with an old friend? Or dropped by someone's house because you were "in the neighborhood"? Or drank beer from a paper bag at 2:00 in the afternoon? Through procrastination, you'll be able to reconnect with the friends that have meant so much to you throughout the years. Your renewed social energy will also lead you to meet new friends, helping you become a better-rounded and -liked person, not to mention providing you with more procrastination partners in crime.

Never Boring

All work and no play makes Jack and Jill pretty dull. If all you do is work, whether taking care of the house, tending to personal hygiene, running after the kids, paying bills, or crunching office deadlines, what else will you have to talk about? Without actively participating in the world—socializing, reading, watching television, surfing the Internet—you become isolated from society and have nothing to contribute to conversations.

You Only Live Once

You're going to die. Yes, reincarnation is a possibility, but it has yet to be definitively proven, so you might as well assume this is your only shot— and if you're wrong, it'll be a nice surprise. To paraphrase the old adage, on your deathbed you won't remember the time you delivered that global-warming report two days early, but you'll certainly be thinking about the day you and your friends mooned the toll-taker during that road trip to Reno.

Everyone's Doing It

Despite the increasing societal pressure to get more done, the number of self-professed procrastinators in the United States has grown steadily over the last few decades, up from about 5 percent in 1978 to 30 percent in 2007. Given the numerous technological and creative advances during the same time period, it appears that the nation still got the job done. Procrastinate *now* to be part of this growing trend—you don't want to be stuck at work while the rest of the country figures it out.

Procrastination Saves Time

Many misguided souls labor under
the misconception that procrastination wastes time, when actually
the exact opposite is true. Instead,
procrastination is one of the keys
to using your time to its maximum

Procrastinators' Hall of Fame: Leonardo da Vinci

In addition to his achievements in art and invention, Leonardo da Vinci was also a well-known
procrastinator. His prolific output is matched
only by his volume of random doodles and
meandering sketches. Leonardo's procrastination secret was his brilliant brain: with so many
interests and skills, he would start one thing and
suddenly be intrigued by something else, leaving the first activity unfinished. His painting was
also subject to top-notch procrastination: the
Mona Lisa took 20 years to finish, for example,
and he never completed the *Adoration of the
Magi*. Leonardo often waited to deliver artwork
until the very last moment, when benefactors
threatened they would cut off the money supply.

potential. As you'll learn in chapter 4, because time expands to fit the task that needs to be done, you have all the time in the world to delay!

Better Work at the Last Minute

Studies show that most people perform more successfully under pressure, delivering stronger results than if they had spread their work out over time. Polished procrastinators swear by their ability to harness the energy, creativity, inspiration, and motivation of the eleventh hour.

Better Health Through Procrastination

Procrastination isn't just fun and productive—it's good for you. A holistic approach to total physical and emotional well-being, procrastination meets a variety of essential needs. Like a mental-health professional, procrastination will teach you to relax and slow down. Like a Xanax or Valium, procrastination will soothe your mind and body. Then, like a fitness instructor, procrastination will give you a rush of energy when it's time to get the job done.

Cardiovascular Fitness

Efficient work causes stress and anxiety, putting your cardiovascular health at risk. Procrastination, on the other hand, will help you maintain a heart-healthy lifestyle. As a practiced procrastinator, you may even fear that your heart is pumping a little too leisurely, but not to worry—soon enough you'll be sprinting to get

The Procrastinator's Creed

1. I believe that if anything is worth doing, it would have been done already.

2. I shall never move quickly, except to avoid more work or find excuses.

3. I will never rush into a job without a lifetime of consideration.

4. I shall meet all of my deadlines directly in proportion to the amount of bodily injury I could expect to receive from missing them.

5. I firmly believe that tomorrow holds the possibility for new technologies, astounding discoveries, and a reprieve from my obligations.

6. I truly believe that all deadlines are unreasonable regardless of the amount of time given.

7. I shall never forget that the probability of a miracle, though infinitesimally small, is not exactly zero.

8. If at first I don't succeed, there is always next year.

9. I shall always decide not to decide, unless of course I decide to change my mind.

10. I shall always begin, start, initiate, take the first step, and/or write the first word when I get around to it.

11. I obey the law of inverse excuses, which demands that the greater the task to be done, the more insignificant the work that must be done prior to beginning the greater task.

12. I know that the work cycle is not plan/start/finish, but wait/plan/plan.

13. I will never put off until tomorrow, what I can forget about forever.

—Anonymous

something done, pumping the beat up so high you may even burn calories.

Relaxation

From the first-time procrastinator to the seasoned expert, almost everyone who practices delay tactics will instantly feel the calming effects associated with taking it easy. Any lingering apprehension over deadlines will quickly subside as you enjoy an *America's Next Top Model* marathon or a long night out with old friends. While die-hard workaholics may assert that procrastination ultimately leads to more stress, instead, as you learn the various skills and techniques to apply procrastination properly, you'll feel a tranquility that will persist during crunch time. With your muscles unwound, the world will seem a much happier, calmer place.

Better Sleep

Scientists are only now uncovering how integral sleep—quality and quantity—is to physical and emotional health. If work keeps you up late at night, stress has you tossing and turning, and you're up at dawn to pack more in, there's no question that your well-being is suffering. Procrastination is without a doubt one of the best ways to assure a better night's sleep—or day's sleep, in the case of napping. *How to Procrastinate* will teach you how to silence the nagging, sleep-stealing voices in your head that pelt you with all the tasks you need to accomplish. Additionally, once you've *decided* to procrastinate on something, rather than deluding yourself that it may in fact get done "tomorrow," you'll find that you stop thinking about it naturally. In no time you'll be passing out in front of the television after a night of cow-tipping with friends, sleeping until noon without a care in the world.

Summer's Glow

Nothing says healthy and happy like a sun-kissed face, an aura you'll never get from fluorescent office lights. Sunshine provides vitamin D, which is essential for health and even cancer prevention. You owe it to yourself—and your tan—to get away from your desk and into the daylight.

Productivity Can Kill

While procrastination benefits your health
in untold ways, you may not yet realize that
efficiency and productivity generate countless negative side effects for both body and
mind. From heart disease to diabetes to
insomnia to inflamed cystic acne, the back-
lash of adhering to schedules, calendars,
and to-do lists can overwhelm even the
most resilient immune system.

Anxiety

Concerns over efficiency cause anxiety, and approximately one in four
Americans will suffer from an anxiety
disorder during his or her lifetime. As
many as 20 percent of all health complaints presented to doctors stem from
anxiety. When you're anxious, your
body experiences a surge of chemicals

through a series of natural reactions
called the "fight or flight" syndrome.
While this chemical burst of strength
is useful when you're being mugged,
it leads to all kinds of health woes if
it happens recklessly and on a consistent basis. The unpleasant symptoms
of anxiety include dizziness, head-
aches, nausea, stomach pains, breathing issues, vision problems, cranki-
ness, heart palpitations, and throat
tightness. Anxiety can also cause
psychological paralysis, rendering you

Jargon of Delay: Hurry Sickness

Condition in which one feels anxiety and frustration due to fear that there is not enough
time to accomplish necessary tasks; causes
stress, heart problems, high blood pressure,
and depression. Coined by cardiologists
Meyer Friedman and Ray Rosenman; they later
renamed the phenomenon "Type A" behavior.

incapable of performing adequately. Finally, with your imagination wrapped up in all the ways you might miss a deadline rather than freely exploring new ideas or song lyrics, fearfulness can hinder your creativity.

Stress

When you're forced to accomplish things, stress is the inevitable result. One of the main hormones secreted during stress, cortisol weakens the immune system, boosts appetite and causes weight gain, induces depression, and raises heart rate, blood pressure, and cholesterol and triglyceride levels. Stress also wreaks gastrointestinal havoc and ranks as the number-one cause of addiction relapse.

Workaholism

Repeated and prolonged productivity can bring on a serious condition called anhedonia—the inability to experience pleasure. When rare moments of leisure arise, workaholics feel they need to get even more done, rendering them incapable of enjoying free time. Not only do all their hobbies, diversions, and relationships atrophy from underuse, these anti-procrastinators are often addicted to the sense of accomplishment that comes from performance.

The Sticky Web of Efficiency

Efficiency is a slippery slope—the more you do, the more you'll be relied upon to accomplish. Because it's encouraged, productivity is all around us, making it difficult—but not impossible—to escape from its grasping talons. As you now understand, however, obligations and expectations will ruin your life. Fortunately, you're about to learn a much better way. Before you jump into procrastination execution, however, it's necessary to take a look at the procrastination mindset. All worthwhile personal change starts above the neck, and in the next chapter, we'll lead you through the psychology of putting things off.

CHAPTER 2
CHANGING YOUR ATTITUDE: FROM "CAN-DO!" TO "WHY NOW?"

THAT THE IDEA OF PROCRASTINATION might scare you is entirely understandable. After all, if you're like most of us, you've been indoctrinated from birth with the misbegotten notion that productivity, promptness, responsibility, and efficiency are the only paths to happiness. Your fear of turning off the phone and turning on the television is based not only on your upbringing but also on macrocosmic social trends. Since the Industrial Revolution, with its specialization of labor and inhuman emphasis on clock-punching, work has increasingly been valued as an end unto itself, a virtue quite separate from the goods or services produced.

In the last 50 years, we've transformed ourselves from cogs in wheels to fingers on keyboards. Each technological innovation has brought not more leisure but instead a heightened perception that we should work all the time. Couple that with the magazines, television shows, and books aimed at helping people "be their best" and "have it all," whether through personal growth, physical fitness, blind religious obedience, improved organization, or, worst yet, the concept of "doing it yourself," and it takes an open mind and independent spirit to buck the tide.

The decision to procrastinate attests to your mental independence. We understand that you may still have a few misgivings, so in this chapter we're going to help you deconstruct them one by one, including:

- Why your longtime belief in efficiency isn't your fault.

- How to overcome anti-procrastination criticism from friends and loved ones.

- Why "I might not get it done if I wait" is *not* an acceptable excuse not to procrastinate.

- What you should never do on New Year's Eve.

Productivity Prejudice

Before you can become an effective procrastinator, it's vital that you overcome any residual anti-procrastinatory guilt. The first step is understanding that you weren't born with the efficiency ethic. As a child, in fact, you had it exactly right—you did nothing but sleep, eat, and relax while someone else wiped your bottom and brought home the bacon. But as you got older, you were told that productivity was important. By recognizing the sources of this destructive mindset, you can quickly overcome these negative thoughts.

Society

As we've already outlined, industrialized countries are notorious for their dictatorship of efficiency, driven by the constant invention of various tools to make you produce and purchase more than you otherwise would. All this fuss over efficiency has increased the value of free time to the point that leisure itself is now referred to as a "luxury." Who wants a life in which your own spare time—something you were born with for free—is a commodity you have to pay for by working?

> ## Historic Procrastination
>
> Derived from the Latin *procrastinatus* (*pro-*, "for," + *crastinus*, "tomorrow"), it was first used in English by lawyer Edward Hall in *The Union of the Two Noble and Illustre Famelies of Lancastre and Yorke*, published in 1548. Clearly not a procrastinator himself, Hall used the word to describe someone productive: "Without longer procrastinacion, he assembled togither."

Family

Our parents want the best for us and thus drive us to succeed. But all too often their definition of success entails productivity and earning a living. We've all seen a soccer mom carting her children from one after-school activity to another—even the kids are overbooked without a second to spare. While her intentions are good, that soccer mom is unwittingly setting her offspring up for a life of stress, anxiety, and punctuality.

Teachers and Bosses

Authority figures demand efficiency. As early as kindergarten, whether at finger-painting or naptime, you've been asked to produce. By college, even though you were paying to attend, professors imposed unreasonable demands on your time—including outside of class, with reading assignments and the like—all under the guise of education. Bosses feel they have the right to dictate how you spend your time just because they pay you. Most authority figures are unreasonable about the demands of your social life, generally resisting any changes to their schedules. Tread carefully here, however. You don't want to spill the beans about your new commitment to procrastination. All these authority figures want is results or a credible excuse (see chapter 9, "The Point of No Return: It's Finally Time to Do Something").

Significant Others

Invoking the argument that what you do involves or reflects on them, significant others can be outspoken when it comes to your procrastination. Lovers and spouses will claim that they're adversely affected by your delaying tactics around career change, home improvement, or quitting smoking. The best way to handle a better half is to involve him or her in your procrastination. All they really want is to be let in on the fun, so offer an invitation to your new friend's kegger, a midnight movie, or your Super Mario Bros. tournament, and soon they'll be on your side! Or, when they say they want to discuss your procrastination with you, put them off.

Popular Efficiency Excuses

We've all been there—faced with a prime procrastination opportunity but foiled by a pro-efficiency excuse. The trick to evicting these common thoughts from your head is understanding why they're wrong.

Deferred Words

"One of the greatest labor-saving inventions of today is tomorrow."

—Vincent T. Foss

When they begin to circulate in your brain, merely remind yourself of the reasons why they lack merit.

"I'm naturally an organized person."

Remember—you weren't born organized; you were *made* organized. Therefore, with a bit of work, you can become disorganized. By uncovering their natural instinct to wait, even the most buttoned-up individuals can learn to procrastinate. Once they experience their newfound freedom, the pleasure of procrastination becomes a self-reinforcing cycle. You'll learn more about this process later (see chapter 3, "Productivity Types: Overcoming Your Natural Inclinations").

"I'd rather just get it over and done with."

Completing a task or project almost always guarantees additional deadlines and more work, meaning you'll never actually finish crossing things off your to-do list. By procrastinating, you'll ensure that your plate never gets too full.

"I might do a better job if I start it now."

Most people work better under pressure, finding more inspiration and creativity than if they'd dedicated unnecessary time. Over half of those who consider themselves to be consistent procrastinators swear by their ability not only to pull off their delayed projects or tasks, but also to do them better than if they'd been dilly-dallying on it all along.

"If I wait, I might not have enough time to finish."

The key to successful procrastination isn't having *enough* time, it's knowing the *right* time. We'll teach you how to wait until just the right point to start doing something unavoidable, and not a moment sooner, ensuring the minimum necessary amount of success not only for your project but also for your life. By paying attention to certain signs (for example, repeated phone messages and threats of being fired), you'll learn to sense the right time to start and finish your tasks.

"My friends and family will disown me."

It's highly likely that you've underestimated your loved ones. If they're worth keeping in your life, what they

Lazy Industry

Author Fred Gratzon has put forth the theory that most of life's progress has been motivated by laziness, not productivity. He points to modern conveniences and technologies, most of which were intended to result in labor *savings*: the dishwasher cleans dishes faster and more easily than a person, the washing machine scrubs clothing more efficiently than a washboard, and what is a modern assembly line if not a mode of easing work? A great deal of economic and social progress can be traced not to the "Can-do" mindset but to the "Why now?" mentality. Therefore, every procrastinator can identify with famous inventors, as the procrastinator's goal is to find ways to create more recreation time for herself.

want most is to see you happy. Until now, the only way they've known to encourage your happiness is to push you toward productivity and earning a gainful living. When you show them how satisfied and relaxed you are with your new lifestyle, not to mention the fact that you'll have more time for them than before, everybody will win.

"I'm getting old!"

It's a cliché, but like most clichés, it's true: age is just a number. Who decided you needed to accomplish something by a certain time? Not you! You're an independent free-thinker, and such benchmarking does nothing but create unrealistic comparisons with others. Gone are the days when someone spent his entire career in one job, when her eggs and marital prospects were dried up at 35; now we can pack many seasons into one lifetime. Forcing yourself along unnatural paths of progression will age you more quickly than anything else. Instead, realize that you'll

do what you need to do when you
need to do it, and in the meantime,
throw another frozen pizza in the
toaster oven.

Managing Expectations

As you ease your way into full-force procrastination, you'll want to pave the road
to putting things off. There are a few
tricks and tips to balancing maximum
procrastination with minimum disappoint-
ment. While a certain amount of letting
yourself and others down is an inevitable
impact of procrastination, in an ideal scenario, you will manage expectations to
your advantage. The skilled procrastinator
always underpromises and underdelivers—
that way, the only surprise is when you *do*
come through!

Avoid Commitments to Others

When you tell people you'll do something, a funny thing happens: they expect you to follow through. Making promises to others quickly leads to a burgeoning to-do list, not to mention disappointed friends, coworkers, and bosses. By sidestepping obligations of any kind, you return time to yourself and make fewer enemies. To avoid commitment, simply look away, change the topic, or end the conversation when someone expects you to step up to the plate. If you find yourself unable to employ these subtle tactics, however, don't feel any qualms about making "pie-crust promises" (easily made and easily broken).

Perma-Student: The Longest Coed Tenure

Undergraduate Johnny Lechner arrived as a freshman at the University of Wisconsin–Whitewater in 1994. Despite several threats to graduate in 2006 or 2007 with a quadruple major and triple minor (areas of emphasis included theater, communications, liberal studies, health, education, women's studies, and social work), Lechner has managed to postpone the inevitable for 13 years. With over 300 credits on his transcript, one can only wonder how many of this 30-year-old's 120 term papers were turned in on time. When asked why he would not graduate in 2007, Lechner said, "Unfortunately, I was living it up just a little bit too much, partying at every major college in the Midwest," and neglected to complete necessary graduation paperwork. The mavens of productivity have cracked down on Lechner's lifestyle, however, with a good dose of procrastination persecution. In 2005, the UW Board of Regents implemented what Lechner calls a "slacker tax." With the reasoning that the state of Wisconsin would only subsidize standard undergraduate education, the board doubled full-time in-state tuition for students who exceed 165 credits.

Avoid Commitments to Yourself

Resolutions and life goals are promises to yourself, and if you make and break them, the only result will be self-loathing. Where's the fun in that? Publishers and product-pushers sell their goods by promising a new, better you. That's impossible, because you're already the best, and only, "you" there is. Even the occasional pledge can harm the budding procrastinator by undoing your hard work spent doing nothing. If you really wanted to lose weight, stop drinking, or get out of debt, you'd have done it by now—and not this January 1.

Carpe Tomorrow

The ultimate motivation to procrastinate is the fact you only live once. Fortunately, all your excuses for getting down to business have been dismantled one by one, freeing you to live the lifestyle you've dreamed about. Now we're going to take this fresh new attitude and use it to examine your functional inclinations toward productivity, identifying what type of efficient worker you are so that we can chart the best path to overcoming your unique personality flaws.

CHAPTER 3
PRODUCTIVITY TYPES: VERCOMING YOUR NATURAL INCLINATIONS

NOW YOU'RE WELL VERSED IN THE pitfalls of efficiency and the benefits of procrastination. To start procrastinating at the highest possible level, however, you must first identify what sort of productive worker you are in order to overcome your natural tendencies accurately and effectively. Though facing one's own shortcomings is never painless, and establishing ways to work through those flaws requires some vigilance, fortunately the transition isn't terribly difficult. After all, if becoming a procrastinator were rocket science, most procrastinators wouldn't be able to do it!

Productivity defects clump into several archetypes. To implement the appropriate antidotes, you'll not only learn about dynamics that distinguish most efficiency mavens, you'll discover which of the following designations best characterizes you:

- The Overachiever

- The Worrier

- The Planner

- The Worker Bee

- The Resolution Maker

Common Productivity Traits

While producers and clock-punchers fall into distinct types, there are some attributes to be found in almost all efficient individuals. You'll want to familiarize yourself with this list in order to recognize and combat the expression of these harmful predispositions:

- **Traditionally productive:** Almost all efficient workers hold the values of traditional productivity, meaning they judge themselves and their work by standards set by society and by authorities such as parents, teachers, and bosses rather than by standards they themselves set.

- **Businesslike:** Many efficient workers pride themselves on their professionalism, viewing the office as a place suitable only for accomplishing work. Additionally, they take this attitude of professionalism into their personal lives, obsessively making good on personal commitments and rarely letting their hair down.

- **Organized:** Organization is a red flag of efficiency. Productive workers tend to rely heavily on the crutchlike trappings of calendars, planners, to-do lists, schedules, and filing supplies. Their desks are frequently clear, or at the very least hold only the neatest presorted piles of papers.

Procrastinators' Hall of Fame: Douglas Adams

Douglas Adams, author of the hugely famous *Hitchhiker's Guide to the Galaxy* series, was a celebrated procrastinator. The *Hitchhiker's* series originated on BBC Radio, and Adams often handed script pages to the radio actors just as they were about to go on the air. Implementing a classic bait-and-switch maneuver (see chapter 7), Adams once put off writing a book by writing a script about not being able to finish a book. In an infringement of Adams's procrastination rights, his book editors once locked him in a hotel room for three weeks so he would complete a manuscript. Adams's favorite procrastination activities were wonderfully sybaritic, and included long, hot baths, preparing and drinking cup after cup of hot tea, and creating and consuming delicious snacks.

- **Systematic:** Due to their repressive inability to go with the flow, productive workers conduct their days methodically, applying repetitive and specific approaches to various tasks. Systematic individuals tend to be flustered by deviations in their schedules and shun spontaneity.

- **Team-oriented:** While there are a few exceptions to this characteristic, especially among back-stabbing, narcissistic executive types, average producers subscribe to a team ethos—whether or not they feel they work better on their own. Some, especially overachievers, assume leadership roles in order to direct teams to be more productive, hence projecting their efficiency needs onto others.

The Five Types of
Productive Workers

While the basic traits you've just learned
about tend to run through all the productive worker types, to gain a deeper
understanding of your own motivations
and inclinations it's important to further
characterize individual manifestations of
efficiency. By identifying which archetype
best describes you, you'll be much closer to
becoming an effective procrastinator.

The Overachiever

The overachiever finds her value in
the regard of others, having learned
at an early age that attention and
acclaim visit those who perform to
exaggerated standards. Rather than
drawing from internal strength, the
overachiever requires outside feedback

for a sense of self-worth. To the over-achiever, nothing is ever enough. One promotion is quickly forgotten in favor of the next advancement. An A could have been an A+. The overachiever is never satisfied, and setting the bar increasingly higher is not only dangerous to the overachiever herself, but also to those around her, since she raises the authority figure's expectations for all team members. In her personal life, the overachiever either focuses on work to the exclusion of other arenas or strives to "have it all" with the perfect spouse, children, cars, house, and social life, but these trappings are merely expressions of her insecurity rather than satisfying pursuits unto themselves.

Procrastination Careers

If you're considering a new way to pay your bills late, you might consider becoming a bank teller, post office clerk, or DMV bureaucrat. Each of these occupations provides ample opportunity for the procrastinator to practice his craft in a procrastination-friendly environment. Practically a PhD in the art of looking busy, these positions offer the chance to check and recheck meaningless documents as well as conduct personal business while others wait.

The pinnacle of professional procrastination, however, belongs to the building trades, including general contractors and any of the subcontracting specialties (especially electricians). The beauty of these industries is that they have no accountability *whatsoever* when it comes to time (or, frequently, to money). They regularly quote 3-month projects that exceed 12! As a contractor, it's acceptable to take on more clients than you can handle (getting deposits from each) and manage the overload by postponement. Your cell phone will go automatically to voicemail, with a cheery message that says you'll call back "as soon as possible" even though you never will. When you do see clients, explain that you have to finish another job, then head to the beach.

Are you an overachiever?

- In school, did you sit in the front row with your hand in the air? Did you complete your homework on time? Did you take advanced-placement classes?

- Did you take part in student government, join the debate team or school band, or participate in team sports?

- Have you won awards at work or at school?

- Do you take on extra projects and work just so you can "learn more"?

- At work, are you in a position of management? Have you gone on to start your own business, or have you become a leader in your field?

- Do you have 2.5 children?

How to overcome: Because you're addicted to accomplishment, you'll want to view procrastination as your latest project and aim to be the best procrastinator ever. Your need for positive feedback from others can be satisfied by dropping your achievement-oriented friends and seeking out other procrastinators so they can positively reinforce your procrastinatory accomplishments.

The Worrier

The worrier feels and internalizes societal pressure, fearing that the world will come to an end if he does not complete tasks both assigned and self-imposed. Where the overachiever is generally confident of her ability to execute but feels driven by the need to do more and better, for the worrier,

quantity and quality are not as
important as avoiding disaster. The
worrier takes to heart every assignment, deadline, task, and project,
motivated by the possibility of a negative outcome. He constantly assesses
whether he will be able to finish on
time and whether his work will be
good enough. Due to his obsessive
nature, the worrier must contend
with the harmful health effects of
stress and anxiety.

Are you a worrier?

- Were you a bed-wetter as a child?

- Do you have dreams about missing
  exams?

- Do you fear disapproval from a
  boss, professor, colleague, or peer?

- Are you afraid you won't be able to get things done on time?

- Do you find yourself obsessing about the consequences of poor performance?

- Do you doubt your ability to do a good job?

- Does your fear drive you to work harder?

How to overcome: Ease into procrastination so you don't inflame your anxieties. You may want to try taking antianxiety medication to free yourself from your own demons and allow your procrastinatory self to blossom. Release your fears by taking baby steps—for example, you could force yourself to miss a minor deadline to demonstrate to yourself that apocalypse does not ensue. Scrutinize authority figures for signs of weakness, and you'll probably realize that they are fallible humans who miss their own deadlines. Once you've unchained yourself from your irrational fear, your ability to procrastinate will snowball!

The Planner

The planner fears losing control and is hence uncomfortable with spontaneity. By imposing order on her (and often others') time, the planner feels a crucial sense of omnipotence. The planner would prefer not to have to think about options or contemplate gray areas, instead relying on her calendar and to-do lists to dictate what she needs to do at any given moment. For the planner, her schedule is the infrastructure of her world; if the infrastructure were to disappear, the whole building would tumble down. Because the planner is likely to be frustrated with procrastinators for their inability to adhere to a schedule, this type will have some initial difficulty in transitioning to successful procrastination.

Are you a planner?

- Do you have a wristwatch tan line?

- Did you know what you wanted to be when you grew up, when you would get married, and what your first child's name would be?

- In school, did you covet the syllabus, comforted by its clear-cut schedule?

- Are you the first to ask when a project or task is due? Do you remind others of deadlines?

- Do you squirm inwardly when others suggest "playing it by ear"?

- Do you love office supplies?

How to overcome: *Plan* your procrastination! Use your calendar and to-do lists to track all the things you'll do to postpone work. Use lined notebooks to make lists of what you could do instead of accomplishing a given task (see chapter 7, "Bait-and-Switch vs. Bonbons: What to Do

Mommy Oldest

Those of you who hear the loud ticking of the bio-logical clock (no matter how much you drink) will be happy to hear that Carmela Bousada of Spain waited until she was 66 to have children, qualify-ing not only as the oldest first-time mother but the oldest mother *ever*! After Bousada's heart was broken years ago, she put off her dreams of children. But when her 101-year-old mother died, the retired department store employee sold her apartment and used the money to pay for sperm and egg donation followed by in-vitro fertilization. Though she had gone through menopause years earlier, Bousada persuaded her Los Angeles fertility doctors that she was only 55, the oldest age the clinic would allow for in-vitro treatment. On December 29, 2006, Bousada gave birth to premature twin boys in Barcelona, 7 days before her 67th birthday.

Instead"). Gradually wean yourself of these crutches, trying to execute one spontaneous procrastination per day. When you feel comfortable in your progress, try going one day without *any* planning. Soon you'll burn your calendars and reminder notes.

The Worker Bee

The worker bee likes to follow orders and keep busy. She prefers an office job with clear-cut parameters and a boss to tell her what to do. She may choose a spouse who will provide a day-to-day life itinerary. The worker bee fears downtime with nothing to do because she lacks confidence in her own decision-making ability; when she is busy and has a task to accomplish, she feels pleasurably productive.

Are you a worker bee?

- Were you an obedient, non-rebellious child with a full roster of household chores?

- Do you offer to take on others' tasks so you will have something to do?

- Would you be happy to follow-through with whatever is decided?

- Do you have a "honey-do" list?

- Do your hobbies consist of house-keeping or home-improvement?

How to overcome: If you're a worker bee, think of procrastination as your new job. View this book as your boss, taking orders from its pages diligently and faithfully. This book is the authority figure, and it is your duty and responsibility to maintain the procrastination tactics outlined here.

The Resolution Maker

Of all the productive types, the resolution maker has the biggest head start on procrastination, as he has a lifetime of experience starting resolutions "next week" and frequently failing to make good on them. The resolution maker typically uses occasions—anniversaries, birthdays, season changes, New Year's Eve—as motivations for grand lifestyle changes. Resolutions are also applied to smaller tasks; for example, promising himself he'll vacuum the house after an hour of television.

Are you a resolution maker?

- When you were a child, did you bargain with your parents about when you would clean your room?

- Do you frequently find yourself using "if-then" statements?

- Do you make grand promises but often neglect to carry through?

- Do you binge-eat during the holiday season?

- Do you often find yourself waiting for something—perhaps an item you feel you need in order to start—before beginning work on a task?

How to overcome: Make a sweeping resolution to procrastinate, then formulate mini-resolutions to accomplish your goals. Rather than aiming to get into shape or be a better parent, set a goal of reading more tabloid magazines, watching more golf, and regularly sleeping in.

Know Thyself, Heal Thyself

You can't change unless you know what you need to change. Hopefully you've seen your own portrait in the five efficiency types and you've come away with some tools for combating your individual self-destructive tendencies. Taking a look in the mirror and facing up to your efficiency can be a difficult process; we commend your courage and assure you that the effort will be worthwhile. Next we'll move from inner-self to outer world as we outline the many overarching principles and scientific theories behind procrastination.

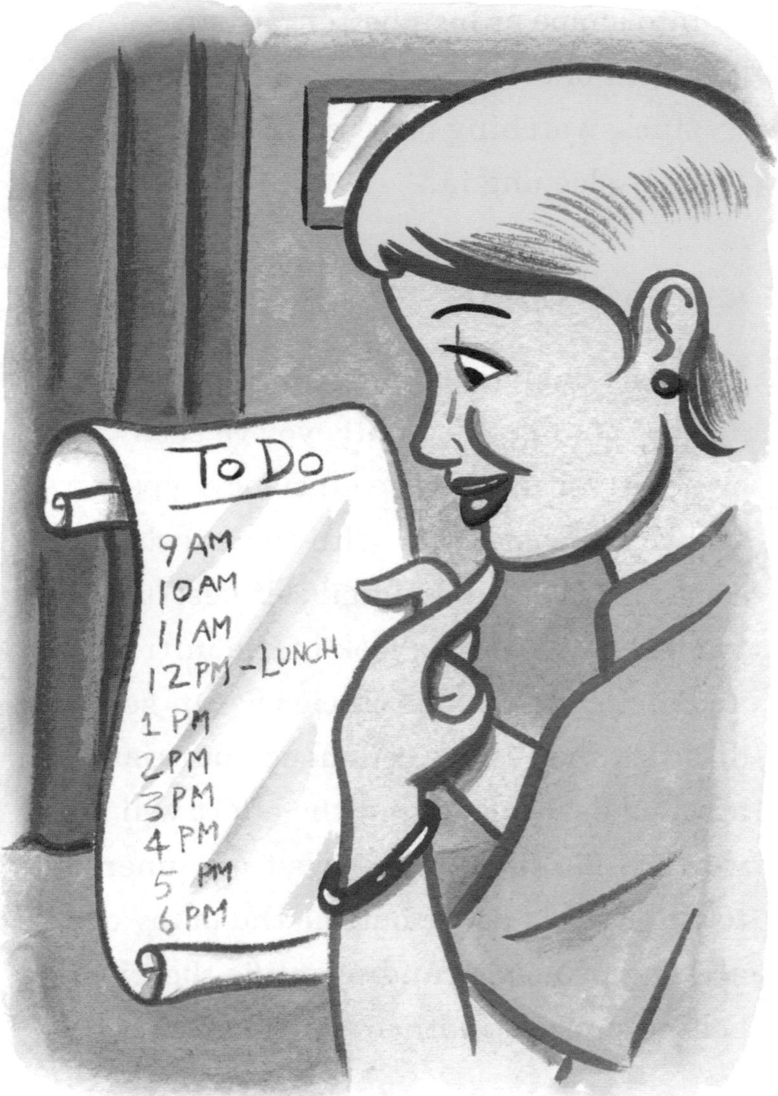
To Do
9 AM
10 AM
11 AM
12 PM - LUNCH
1 PM
2 PM
3 PM
4 PM
5 PM
6 PM

CHAPTER 4
NIVERSAL PROCRASTINATION DYNAMICS: TIME IS A HUMAN INVENTION

CONTRARY TO POPULAR BELIEF, THE expert procrastinator is not unaware of time. While non-procrastinators let time control them, skilled procrastinators control time, twisting it to their advantage. Before you can make time work for you, you must first grasp how time actually works. Only then will you harness its power and make the jump from efficiency to delay.

In this chapter, you'll learn to discard all trappings of time—your watch, your calendar, your alarm clock. You'll take back your time by choosing to do what you want, when you want. No matter how chained to a schedule you may now be, soon you will own your own time.

While much of the material in this chapter may initially sound a little complicated, you only need to understand the gist of it, and might even learn something to discuss over cocktails with friends or ponder during a Pink Floyd Laserium show—while procrastinating, of course. Concepts in this chapter include:

- Why time is a human-made invention.

- How Parkinson's Law proves you must wait to begin a project.

- How to calculate the ratio of motivation to procrastination.

- When you should start work in the morning—and whether you should start *any*thing in the morning.

A Brief History of Time

No lesser light than Albert Einstein once said, "Space and time are modes by which we think, not conditions under which we live." Historians believe the Cro-Magnons were the first to record time, more than 30,000 years ago, using phases of the moon to mark days, weeks, months, and years. Egyptians divided the day into 24 hours, and the Greeks defined the hour. The sundial, the first timepiece, became popular around 3500 BCE, as did other primitive time-measurers such as water clocks and hourglasses. You can tell all the clock-punchers out there that clocks weren't even invented until the thirteenth century—imagine how easy it was to procrastinate back then!

Clearly time is a human invention, a concept that philosophers and scientists have long debated. As an aspiring procrastinator, if time were real, you'd be battling a natural force as strong as a hurricane or tidal wave. Since time is relative, however, and because $E = MC^2$, the diligent procrastinator can wrangle time into submission.

THEORIES OF TIME

While there are many laws and theories that explicate time, three in particular are most useful for the aspiring procrastinator:

Parkinson's Law

Formulated in 1955 by scholar C. Northcote Parkinson, Parkinson's Law states that "work expands so as to fill the time available for its completion." That means that if you start your project early or "on time," as time is traditionally defined, you'll end up having performed more work than if you had waited until the last possible second. Here's an example: if you're assigned a report to write, and given 2 weeks, you could work on it every day for 4 hours, ultimately investing 40 hours (given the 5-day workweek) in the project. However, if you do it the night before, you only spend 6 to 8 hours, for a procrastinator's profit of at least 32 hours. Who wouldn't like an extra 32 hours to do whatever they choose?

The knack to applying this principle, however, is knowing exactly *when* to start working, leaving enough time to get the job done with the bare minimum of effort (see chapter 9, "The Point of No Return: It's Finally Time to Do Something").

Unfortunately, when you stop to contemplate Parkinson's Law, it's easy to spin into dismay at the realization of how much of your life you've wasted adhering to schedules set by others. Starting as soon as they tell you to begin, you let your work expand to fill days, weeks, months, when you could've easily completed the same amount of work in far less time and spent the rest on the *People* magazine crossword puzzle.

Temporal Motivation Theory

Drawing on some 25 years of research on procrastinatory phenomena, University of Calgary business professor Piers Steel distilled procrastination into one simple theory in "The Nature of Procrastination: A Meta-Analytic and Theoretical Review of Quintessential Self-Regulatory Failure." Steel based his formula on the desirability of completing a task:

Utility = (E × V) / (G × D)

Utility = Desirability of the task.

E = Perceived odds that the task will be successful.

V = How rewarding the outcome will be.

G = Person's "sensitivity to delay."

D = Delay, or length of time between present moment and reward for completed task.

The equation can be calculated at any moment in time and charted on an X-Y axis. Let's calculate the example of a bride attempting to lose weight for her wedding day. Her boyfriend proposes on December 31, and her wedding will take place over Labor Day weekend. While she wants to lose weight, she also enjoys food. Early in her engagement, in moment-to-moment decisions, food is more rewarding to her than weight loss. As the wedding day approaches and she realizes she may not fit into her dress, however, weight loss becomes more rewarding than food. The tipping point—or the point at which weight loss becomes more desirable than eating—is July 5, after she sees photographs of herself in a bathing

suit from the Fourth of July weekend.
With less than eight weeks to go, the
bride gets down to business:

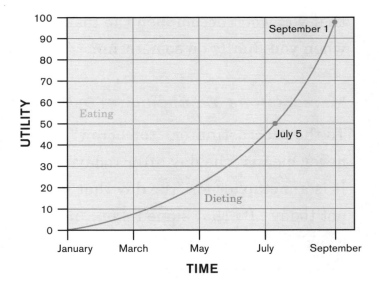

One interesting aspect of Steel's
theory is the incorporation of self-
confidence, or perceived odds that
the task will be successful. Just as
confidence is key to a successful life,

so will this type of optimism increase the quality of your procrastination. What's the point of procrastinating if you're going to worry the whole time that you won't accomplish the task when you finally do something?

Metaphoric vs. Chronological Dating

To the procrastinator, "tomorrow" never means "the day after today." It is a metaphor for "the day that is not today." By that same token, "next week" and "next month" rarely refer to what you can tangibly identify on a calendar. Like an uncompleted task on an electronic calendar that carries over, interminably, to the next day, the procrastinator's tomorrow will never come. These phrases are merely ways the procrastinator indicates a task's degree of presence in his or her mind as well as likelihood that it will ever get done.

The Procrastination Theory of Relativity

This theory is simple: all procrastination is relative. When you have a boring book to read for school, nothing feels more urgent than giving your home a good spring cleaning. The

---

Why Even Start?

Douglas Hofstadter, author of the Pulitzer prize–winning *Gödel, Escher, Bach: An Eternal Golden Braid*, created the paradoxical and all-too-true Hofstadter's Law, which states, "It always takes longer than you expect, even when you take into account Hofstadter's Law." It's therefore impossible ever to calculate or recalculate the time needed to complete a task because the law is recursive—meaning it refers to itself. Therefore, as with the half-life of radium or high school algebra, calculations are asymptotic: they accelerate toward an axis without ever reaching it.

---

cleaning is the procrastination, while the book is the task. Let's say, however, that the book is the latest pot-boiler from your favorite author. Your parents are coming to town in a couple of days, and the house must be clean before they arrive. In that scenario, clearly, the book is the procrastination and the cleaning is the task. Ergo, procrastination is relative.

Baby Steps

We understand that all of this may seem a bit overwhelming for the emerging procrastinator. These time theories are not only intellectually challenging, they fly in the face of the clock-driven life you've needlessly led. Be assured, however, that the manipulation of time is completely feasible. Some of you will need to take concrete, small

Event Time vs. Clock Time

In his book *A Geography of Time*, sociology professor Robert Levine notes how various cultures define and contemplate time differently. Industrialized societies tend to use what Levine calls "clock time": appointments are scheduled and durations are measured by the clock. Non-industrialized cultures, however, tend to use "event time," based on the organic rhythm of activities and popular consensus. Events don't start until they start and take as long as they take. Event time can be synchronized with nature—for example, sunset rather than 6:00 PM. Some cultures, Levine notes, don't even have a single word to express the concept of time!

steps before tackling larger time-manipulation projects. Here are a few simple ways to easily bend the hours in your favor:

- Don't get started right away when you arrive at work (late) each morning. Instead, bring your breakfast, read the paper, IM with your buddies. Whether it takes five minutes or five hours, don't get started until you're good and ready.

- If someone asks you when you'll have something done, be as vague as possible in response, refusing to pin yourself down to a deadline.

- Always leave the house with far less time than you'll need to arrive punctually. If you keep yourself busy until the time of departure, you'll be too distracted to worry about being late, and then you'll be late no matter what!

Jargon of Delay: Time Porn

Situation found in many sitcoms, such as *Friends* and *Seinfeld*, in which attractive characters seem to have nothing to do but spend leisure time hanging out with friends. If they have jobs at all, hours required are apparently minimal.

As you get into the swing of the infinite array of procrastination tactics, you'll learn to spot opportunities for time delay in almost every assignment or task.

What Time Is It? Who Cares!

Time pressures and the perceived lack of time are among the novice procrastinator's greatest complaints. As you've seen, however, time is merely a figment of the human imagination, and, as an increasingly expert procrastinator, you can bend time at will. But to what activities should you apply these hard-won skills? In the next chapter, we'll explore which responsibilities you should put off right away—and which ones you should put off putting off until later.

CHAPTER 5

)ROP THAT FILE AND GRAB THE REMOTE!
ACTIVITIES TO PUT OFF

LIFE IS FILLED WITH DELAY-WORTHY tasks, projects, and personal transformations. Pre-procrastinators often reflexively feel that they need to accomplish things, and this chapter will focus on those tasks you've previously felt compelled to complete. Not only will we demonstrate how to drag your feet, we'll reveal the risks of attempting these foolish goals and the benefits you'll reap by procrastinating each and every time. You'll learn:

- The damaging downside of turning projects in on time.

- The best ways to put off paying taxes and bills.

- How you can always lose weight tomorrow.

- Why dating, relationship improvement, and procreation should be delayed.

School Assignments

If you're a student, it's fair to assume that you're already ahead in the procrastination game. Though procrastination is a learned skill, among the general population students come closest to being natural procrastinators. For those students not paying their way through school, perhaps they procrastinate so successfully because the stakes are lower than in adulthood. For younger students, living at home affords certain securities and useful targets against which to rebel—a form of delay known as "reactionary procrastination."

Whether in high school, college, or graduate school, working to meet academic goals holds you back from the most important aspect of education: socializing. Social pursuits provide self-understanding as well as knowledge of the larger world: meeting people from other cultures and religions, comparing Thai lager to Indian pilsner. Keeping your nose to the grindstone will only cause you to miss out on the parties, mixers, and bar nights that would introduce you to the *real* world. If you leave your education to the discretion of teachers and textbooks, you'll leave school a shallow, closed-minded automaton with an immature liver.

In a survey conducted for this book, 55 percent of respondents began practicing procrastination in college, once released from their parents' watchful thumbs, while 15 percent used college as a way to hone procrastination skills they already possessed. And those who went on for PhDs and wrote a dissertation? Forget about it—those individuals are the master procrastinators of all time. The lesson is clear: as you embrace procrastination, always let the other students be your teacher.

Work Projects

Work can be enjoyable, if only for the coffee breaks and gossip, but it also entails deadlines and responsibilities, leaving you subject to the whims of an (often unqualified) authority figure. While it would be best not to have a job at all, it's an unfortunate necessity for most of us. If you're not careful, however, work will overtake you entirely. The goal for any procrastinator is work to live, not live to work. Translation? Do the bare minimum necessary to support a procrastinatory lifestyle.

Deferred Words

"Anyone can do any amount of work, provided it isn't the work he is supposed to be doing at that moment."
—Robert Benchley

By practicing punctual go-getterism, you will unleash a chain reaction of negatives. If you turn something in early once, it will be expected thereafter. If you finish your work efficiently, more will be heaped onto your plate. If you show competence, the untended tasks of other procrastinators will be transferred to you. We remind you that one of the procrastinator's most basic mantras is "underpromise and underdeliver."

A procrastinatory employee rarely takes initiative, hedges when asked to commit on deadlines, and complains of unforeseen obstacles when asked to turn something in on time. On due dates, the procrastinator calls in sick. If requested to take on another project, the procrastinator recites the litany of current responsibilities. When asked what the problem is, the procrastinator protests, taking great offense at the suggestion of malfeasance or inefficiency. Upon your implementation of these techniques, at a certain point your boss will find it too problematic and unsatisfying to approach you at all. This is advanced and self-perpetuating procrastination at its best, for you have successfully moved away from your association with the go-tos to forever be lumped with the avoid-whenever-possibles.

Of course, the office isn't a complete waste of time. Before the advent of the Internet, working procrastinators had little to distract them from the tasks they attempted to avoid. Work was so boring that even the most committed procrastinators sometimes ended up executing assigned tasks just to relieve the ennui. Now, however, eight hours' worth of entertainment is not only available at the click of a mouse, the fun actually *lives* on your work tool, the computer, rendering it laughably easy to make it appear that you're getting things done.

Home Maintenance

In the Temporal Motivation Theory outlined in chapter 4, one element of the equation is perceived likelihood of success. When it comes to home maintenance, this value equals zero. One definition of crazy is doing the same thing over and over again but expecting a different result, and keeping up with your house is a never-ending process. Whether it's mowing the lawn, cleaning the gutters, or patching the roof, these jobs will crop up no matter how much

Student Syndrome

Coined by author Eliyahu Goldratt in his book *Critical Chain*, "student syndrome" is named after the phenomenon whereby a student asks for an extension on his paper based on the reasoning that the extra time will allow him to do a better job. Despite the extension, the student will be distracted by other responsibilities and will end up writing the paper at the last possible minute. The dynamic can be generalized as using up one's planned buffer or reserve time before work even begins rather than keeping it for unforeseen circumstances.

effort you expend. In two weeks, the lawn will once again need mowing, the gutters will be filled, and the roof will be leaking. You'll *never* be done.

So why start? Those who submit to the rigors of home maintenance usually do so on the weekends. But what are weekends for? Relaxation! You'll never be happy if you take care of your home. While home emergencies are unavoidable, it's best to wait until they occur, then call a professional.

Personal Finances

The personal finance arena offers a wealth of socially acceptable ways to procrastinate; no one wants to handle their money, and almost everyone will understand why you haven't. It's practically patriotic to avoid doing your taxes. If we tend to put off what's least pleasurable, then taxes ranks right up there with dental work. While we're led to believe that April 15 is the annual tax deadline, an extension is easily secured.

When it comes to bill paying, all you need to know is which bills must be paid on time and forget the rest. It's a good idea to promptly pay your mortgage, as late payments will affect your credit rating; however, if you set this up as an automatic bill pay, you'll never have to think about it again. It's no problem to procrastinate with utility bills, which will start coming in red or pink envelopes if there's any danger of shut-off. Since there are many people out there who don't pay at all, most companies are surprisingly happy to have you pay late rather than never.

Self-Improvement

Want to lose weight? Quit smoking? Learn a new language? Save money? In today's self-help-crazed society, it's tempting to set personal goals just to keep up with the Joneses. The root of this problem isn't your inability to live up to these standards—it's the standards themselves, the repressive rule of judgmental perfectionism that has models bingeing in secret then sticking their fingers down their throats, 20-somethings joining gyms they never attend, business travelers covering the latest Tom Clancy novel with a *7 Habits* dust jacket. The drive for self-improvement leads to only one thing: self-loathing.

If you're not perfect just the way you are, why wake up in the morning? If you can fit into commercially available clothing, there's no need to lose weight. With five credit card offers in the mail a day, who saves? Everybody in the world speaks English, and everything you need to know will show up on television eventually. Self-improvement takes time and money, and it's entirely unnecessary. The self-loathing procrastinator is an unhappy procrastinator. The last thing you should do is work hard to become a procrastinator in order to gain personal time only to waste it on negative internal monologues. Far better to spend your extra hours eating pizza and playing video games.

Dating

With the proliferation of Internet dating, romantic socialization has become a job. Writing your profile, taking a picture, responding to email, experiencing rejection and your own lack of interest, endlessly primping beforehand, wishing you were home in front of the television rather than on yet another go-nowhere date—perhaps it would be better if you just stayed home and watched *Desperate Housewives* as you wanted to do in the first place.

By shunning dating, you'll continue to be responsible only for yourself and are less likely to acquire an anti-procrastination

> ## It's Never Too Late
>
> Stephen Sampogna recently returned an over-
> due copy of *The Complete Sherlock Holmes* to
> his Maryland high school library—43 years late.
> Rather than getting in trouble, however, Samp-
> ogna was celebrated in the news and the library
> not only forgave his $152.70 in fines but also
> created an exhibit in his honor. The sign above
> the exhibit? "It's Never Too Late."

significant other. You'll make fewer promises
that you don't intend to keep, allowing you all
the time in the world to do whatever it is you
would rather do. The mental stress of dating
(i.e., "Will she call? Are we going out again?")
can turn even the most delightful of procrastinatory activities into a cacophony of internal distress. Few dates have the potential to
end in marriage, one of the main motivations
behind dating. And a successful date can
open the door to questions of marriage and
children, two areas of life better postponed.

Working on Your Relationship

If you're not fortunate enough to be single as you read this book, you've probably contemplated various sorts of relationship improvement, whether spending quality time together, talking about "us," or entering marriage counseling. Many people are naturally inclined to postpone these activities, a natural procrastination tendency that is to be applauded. The truth is that all such effort absorbs time and energy for questionable return.

Perhaps you've been thinking of having a "date night" with your partner every Friday. Not only is this time-consuming, but when you concentrate solely on each other you may start to notice things you don't like. Did he always have those nose hairs? Did she always laugh a little too loudly? With the high probability of divorce, it's probably not smart to invest time and money into counseling.

Whether or not your efforts would prove successful, the procrastinator always prefers the status quo. The quiet tension and distance you may currently be feeling is the devil you *do* know, whereas communication and emotions are the devil you *don't* know. Always postpone the devil you don't know.

Procreation

Children are the ultimate suckers of time and money, and thus should be postponed for as long as gynecologically possible. It used to be that women who didn't bear children in their twenties and early thirties were less inclined to succeed beyond the age of 35. Thanks to advances in medical

Procrastinators' Hall of Fame: John Huston

Director John Huston couldn't stand to put the finishing touches on a film and tinkered until the very last minute. He continued editing *The African Queen*, starring Humphrey Bogart and Katharine Hepburn, until a few days before its premiere on December 23, 1951. In order to be eligible for an Academy Award nomination, a movie must run for at least seven consecutive days in a Los Angeles theater within the preceding year—and December 23 is considered the cutoff date. On December 23 of the following year, Huston was still editing *Moulin Rouge*, finishing only hours before its Oscars eligibility would have expired. With the good fortune of a skilled procrastinator, Huston was nominated for Best Director for both films.

knowledge and technology, this deadline is pushing later and later in order to accommodate procreative procrastinators. The longer you wait to have kids, the more time you'll have to procrastinate.

If It Matters, Postpone It

Life is a circus, and there are too many rings to keep all the elephants on their hind feet at once. If you try, you'll fail, and worse, you won't enjoy yourself. Whether you're tending to your professional or personal life, you always want to do as little as possible, as late as possible. Flip-flop the old adage "Too little, too late" into "Little enough? Late enough?" and you've got the right idea. In the next chapter, we'll explore ways to address your environment to set it up for maximum procrastination along with some helpful techniques to defer worry and work.

CHAPTER 6

SOME NEW "WORK" HABITS: STAGING PROCRASTINATION

WHEN ADOPTING ANY NEW HABIT, it's important to create an environment and a routine to support the endeavor until it's fully taken root. For your next step as a fledgling procrastinator, you will take a good look at the settings in which you currently toil, rearranging them to postpone work as well as promote your procrastinatory activities. Additionally, you'll learn which activities and tools to avoid along with those that will help advance your effort.

Take a look around your current work environments. Is there a calendar hanging on the wall? Is your in-box empty? Have you crossed completed items off your to-do list?

Are your paperclips sorted by size? If you've answered yes to any of these questions, you'll want to pay especially close attention to this chapter. You'll learn to leave behind the trappings of productivity in order to fully embrace procrastination, transforming your workspace into a slack space in no time at all. We'll review such topics as:

- How to create the charmingly oxymoronic "procrastinator's to-do list."

- What to do with papers instead of filing them.

- Why OOTO is your friend.

- Why corporate lingo will help get you off the hook.

- When to turn on your computer if you work at home.

Clearing Your Desk

Since most of our work is done at our desks, and indeed desks were created for the sole purpose of doing work, this is the best place to start rearranging for procrastination. Even one or two of these changes will nurture your transformation from a doer into a twiddler.

Calendars and Planners

Chuck them. Easily two of the biggest enemies of procrastination, calendars and planners do little more than separate your day into short intervals aimed at keeping you busy. Do you already know what you're doing between 10:00 and 11:00 on the morning of May 11? If the answer is yes, you'd better shred or burn your planner instead of merely throwing it away. Get in the habit now of not keeping track of important days and events. When everyone else is scrambling around because of a deadline, you'll have peace of mind.

To-Do Lists

To-do lists are inventories of time burglary. They do little more than force you into an efficient mindset by taunting you with things that could be done were you so inclined, minor accomplishments that non-procrastinators need in order to call the day, week, or month a success. If it's important enough, you'll remember it later, or someone will remind you. The to-do list habit is an especially hard one to break. Fortunately, there are a couple of helpful tricks: replace boring, work-oriented tasks with fun activities, like catching a movie. Or, add items you've already completed (today, yesterday, a year ago) in order to cross them off for a day well spent.

Desk Accessories

There are entire brands, retail chains, and "experts" devoted to the questionable goal of keeping a neat, productive desk. This is fraud akin to selling bottled water when tap is safe enough to drink: you don't need it. In-boxes are the enemy, giving people a place to put the work they've assigned to you. If it's empty, your boss will think you don't have enough to do. If it's full, she'll think you haven't done enough. Pen cups will deprive you of the "I don't have a pen" excuse, while message boards are nothing more than vertical to-do lists. The only acceptable desk accessories for the procrastinator are staplers, tape dispensers, and Post-its: they make you appear productive, but nobody expects you to actually do anything with them.

Home Offices

Whether or not you work from home, you must not set up a home office. If you've already got one, start using it as a junk room for storing all the items that have no other dedicated place in the house. Soon enough you won't be able to get into the room, let alone sit down at the desk. By taking away a home work environment, you won't necessarily be restricting your-self from doing any work at home. After all, if you work from home, every once in a while you'll have to invoice somebody. Instead, you'll create prime opportunities to procrastinate while you work by setting your laptop up in front of the television, at the kitchen table, or in bed. If the spot you pick is essentially unsuitable for your type of work, you'll be less inclined to accomplish things.

Shunning Organization

Organization is the hallmark of an efficient worker, and therefore must be avoided. Because it takes work to be organized, however, it's easy to be *dis*organized: all you have to do is nothing.

Don't File—Pile!

Lose the folders and the label maker, and use the filing cabinet to store old magazines or hide piles. One of the best things about being a procrastinator is that filing becomes a thing of the past. Instead, create small piles of papers, stacked and grouped in no particular order. Over time, the piles will grow, and they'll naturally evolve into complete disorder—rendering you incapable of acting on anything, forcing you into procrastination.

Don't Name or Save Anything Digital

When it comes to work, the computer is just another big filing cabinet. If you wanted to organize your electronic documents, you'd have to spend time and mental energy on naming protocols, folder hierarchies, and servers. Instead, try to avoid saving at all, and if you must, give the document a name you won't be able to remember later, a moniker that's completely unrelated to the document's subject and purpose. Again—if you can't find it, you can't act on it.

Lose the Daily Routine

While this may seem contrary to the inculcation of a new habit, in order to develop your procrastination skills, you'll want to avoid a daily schedule. Opt instead for spontaneity over rigor. Sunny outside? Go to the beach, the park, or an open-air café. Rainy? Go to the movies. Neither rainy nor sunny? Grab a bite to eat. Every possible contingency represents an occasion to mix it up. Before long, spontaneity will become a natural instinct, and you won't be able to plan anything even if you try.

Tools for Nonproductivity

Thanks to the electronic revolution, there are more tools available to the procrastinator than ever before. A small investment, whether by you or by your employer, will pay off big once you seem like you're working even when you're not. Some of these tools will be surprising to the aspiring procrastinator, as they are implements of work. With the startling exception of the Allen wrench, there is no such thing as a bad tool, only bad usage, and everything in the following list can be used for productivity *or* procrastination.

Telephone

Whether cell phone, voicemail, or caller ID, today's telephone technology, rather than impeding the procrastinator, is actually an unprecedented boon. With a cell phone, you can be reached anywhere, should you so choose, and avoid blame for not being in the "right" place. Only *you* know where you are, and that's the way it should be. With caller ID, you can send selected calls to voicemail, then forget to return the calls or do so at a convenient time for you.

Jargon of Delay: Virtual Friday

The day before a long weekend begins, i.e., if there is no school or work on Friday, Thursday becomes your "virtual Friday." The Wednesday before Thanksgiving can also be termed a virtual Friday.

Though you will rarely answer your phone, voicemails will alert you to any urgent obligations or tasks without your having to remember them. You'll be honest when you say "I had no idea that deadline was today." (In chapter 9, "The Point of No Return: It's Finally Time to Do Something," we'll outline all manner of excuses.) If you must be responsible to a landline, call-forwarding will send calls right to your mobile. And text-messaging allows you to communicate without talking at all, with no lost points for abbreviations and poor spelling.

Laptop Computer

As the cell phone enables you to be reached—or voicemailed—wherever you choose to procrastinate, so does the laptop computer, allowing you to choose your own office, whether your living room or the local bar. Wireless Internet is a must at home, and you'll no doubt find a few such resources outside the house. As a procrastinator, you want to be able to surf the Internet whenever and wherever.

Email

Because it's easily deferred, email is a preferred mode of procrastinatory communication. For a phone call, both participants must be present in the moment. With email, you can attend to an issue whenever you like. Additionally, email affords many technologically derived excuses (see chapter 9).

One underused email utility is the automatic out-of-the-office (OOTO) message. While most people use OOTO messages only for vacations and business trips, they can be harnessed elegantly for the powers of procrastination. You can automatically announce that you're working on a big project, or away on assignment for the day, and indicate either a specific date after which you will begin responding or merely state "as soon as possible." Nobody will expect your reply any sooner!

Foolproof Inefficiency Techniques

Whether you're at home or in the office, it's important to cultivate activities that make you seem like you're working when you're actually procrastinating. Alternatively, you need excuses to spontaneously duck out as well as reasons why you're unavailable.

Remember—a prepared procrastinator is a successful procrastinator.

Looking Busy

Appearing to keep a busy schedule will not only reassure your boss that you're on the job, it will likely shield you from being assigned additional tasks. Here are some simple, time-proven techniques:

- Pick up the phone when your boss walks by, pretending to be on a business call. Adopt a brisk, businesslike tone.

- Carry around a clipboard.

- Accelerate your hallway walking speed in those moments where you would prefer not to stop and chat; look purposeful.

Procrastinators' Hall of Fame: Samuel Taylor Coleridge

British poet Samuel Taylor Coleridge almost never delivered work when it was promised, despite his publishers' pleas. Most famously he wrote part of the poem "Kubla Khan" only to be distracted by a knock at the door. When he returned to finish the poem, he felt he'd lost the mindset (an opium-based hallucination)—and never got around to completing it. The unfinished "Kubla Khan" nonetheless stands as one of literature's best-known poems.

- If you're casually chewing the fat with a friend and others look suspicious, both of you should review a piece of paper and occasionally nod.

- Send blank pieces of paper through the fax machine.

- Print out anything you'd like to read (for personal pleasure) on 8.5-by-11-inch sheets of paper, then pore

over the documents at your desk.
Make notes and use a highlighter.

Food and Coffee

Even bosses have stomachs and
pounding caffeine-deprivation head-
aches, so hunger and the need for
coffee will always get you out of the
office. Offering to pick up coffee for
others will win you friends who will
be more likely to cover for you while
you're out. If you're working at home,
a trip to the kitchen can turn into
a half-hour with a magazine or an
affectionate tumble with the dogs.
Whether or not you're hungry or need
coffee, say you are and you'll get out
of almost any moment.

Buzzwords

Every field has buzzwords, and if you toss them around enough, people will think you're actually working. "Research and development" (R & D) will cover just about any expedition. If you work in sales, say you're conducting "informal focus groups" when you take an afternoon off to get loaded with friends. If you're a writer, you're "researching your demographic" when you go to the movies, take a long people-watching lunch, or hit the local Foot Locker for some new kicks. Maybe you work in technology? Sounds like a great reason to spend the morning briefing yourself on the web traffic to your favorite sites.

"Working" from Home

Working from home or telecommuting constitutes a special type of procrastination environment and as such merits dedicated discussion. For the procrastinator, working from home is ideal. Not only are the distractions more pleasurable, the physical distance and lack of visibility between yourself and your colleagues mean you can do whatever you want without resorting to subterfuge. To make the most of this environment, implement the following techniques:

- Leave the computer off. You can't do work if the screen's dark, and you won't

---

Deferred Words

"I don't think necessity is the mother of invention—invention, in my opinion, arises directly from idleness, possibly also from laziness. To save oneself trouble."

—Agatha Christie

---

be distracted by email alerts. Turn it on just a few times a day to see if anything's urgent.

- Work in front of the television. While you'll be somewhat productive, it won't be efficient.

- Eat lunch in front of the television. You'll get involved in a show and lunch will go over the time you would otherwise have allotted to it.

- Start watching soap operas. Soon you'll be addicted, and the procrastination will carry its own momentum.

- Let friends know you enjoy drop-ins. Spontaneous social visits will break up your load.

- Practice nomadism. If you're not enjoying your work, perhaps the setting is

the problem. A café? The backyard? A
nightclub? The time you spend packing
up and moving from place to place will
effectively whittle into your work time,
and before you're even settled in one
place, you'll crave another.

Working at Procrastination

Whether you work at procrastination or
procrastinate at work, the end result is the
same: success. You may be paid to put in
a certain number of hours at the office, but

management doesn't control your mind—
yet. As you've seen, there are so many ways
to make it appear as if you're working.
What we haven't explored yet is what to do
while you're procrastinating, but never fear,
because it's a beautiful world of possibility.

CHAPTER 7

BAIT-AND-SWITCH vs. BONBONS: WHAT TO DO INSTEAD

ALL PROCRASTINATION ACTIVITIES break down into one of two categories: bait-and-switch or bonbons-and-television. Additionally, procrastinators themselves tend to hew more to one side or the other, so it might be said that these are also procrastinator types. In this chapter, you'll learn the difference between the two and diagnose your own tendencies. We'll remind you that procrastination is relative (remember chapter 4?) and show you that chances to procrastinate flourish all around you: in your home, at the office, and out in the world. Among the concepts you'll learn are:

- Why cleaning the house can be a procrastinator's dream.

- The beauty of mail-order for procrastinatory diversions.

- Cooking and its ability to eat up an entire day.

- How exploring other talents through procrastination can lead to a whole new career.

The Old Bait-and-Switch

This classic form of procrastination actually also qualifies as a form of productivity, but don't let that discourage you. The bait-and-switch (BS) takes the Procrastination Theory of Relativity at its word (see chapter 4, "Universal Procrastination Dynamics: Time Is a Human Invention"). BS is

defined as doing something ostensibly productive *other than what you are supposed to
be doing.*

As a type, BS procrastinators are often
driven by guilt and a vestigial work ethic,
practicing BS in part because they can't
enjoy the bonbons-and-television approach.
The BS procrastinator can only delay a
pivotal and important task by doing other
work that is productive but non-urgent,
despite the necessity of finishing the first
task. Their internal voices simply cannot
accept lack of productivity.

When you're employing BS procrastination in the office, you'll frequently conduct
email correspondence rather than further-
ing a big project. If you've taken reading
home with you, you clean the house. If
you've been told that the garage must be

cleaned and organized *this* weekend or else bedroom privileges will be withheld, in the course of perusing the garage, you'll notice that the fly-fishing tackle box is completely out of sorts and must be set right before the garage can even be contemplated.

Bonbons-and-Television

The opposite of BS procrastination is the bonbons-and-television model (BBTV). BBTV consists of doing something fun and completely unproductive instead of doing what you're supposed to be doing, and as such is the truest form of procrastination. Whether going out for a bar night or putting a dent in the couch, spooning dulce de leche into your mouth, and catching up on *Law and Order* reruns, BBTV tends to involve some form of major mental distraction from the productive tasks at hand.

Naptime

Take a procrastination lesson from the animal kingdom with these ambitious snoozers:

Animal	Sleep*
Koala	22
Sloth	20
Bat	20

Animal	Sleep*
Armadillo	19
Opossum	19
Lemur	16

*Hours per day of sleep.

Rather than making any pretense of doing productive work as BS does, BBTV seeks to block out the knowledge of any other responsibilities, sometimes through the use of reality-altering substances. If you're not naturally inclined to BBTV, you'll have to be very advanced in your procrastination practice to employ it without feeling guilty.

In the Home

Being at home provides the procrastinator with a full array of both BS and BBTV activities. Home is probably the easiest locale in which to enjoy something other than what you're supposed to do, and you don't even have to put on clothes to do it. If you're a student, a telecommuter, or a freelancer, most of your procrastination will likely take place at home where, because you control both environment and time, your range of options is wide.

Housekeeping

Housework is the classic BS procrastination activity not only because it's productive, satisfying, and manageable, but also because it's immensely absorbing. When you're moving quickly and increasing your heart rate, perhaps with loud music playing, it's easy to pull your focus away from what you're supposed to be doing. The movement of housekeeping also provides an outlet for any nervous energy. Housework affords the opportunity to run into an as-yet-untackled organization project, such as cleaning out a closet, that will absorb hours of time, make a big mess at first that must be cleaned up before moving on to anything else, and which may also necessitate the purchase of new organizational accessories (very appealing for the BS procrastinator). Among the top choices for housekeeping procrastination are:

- Dishes, especially if there are just a few in the sink.

- Watering plants.

- General straightening up, such as folding clothes or recycling old newspapers and magazines.

- Laundry, especially sheets and bedcovers.

- Rearranging furniture and electronics.

- Shelving CDs, DVDs, or books, sampling them as you alphabetize.

Television

Unlike housework, television is pure BBTV. One of the most important inventions in the history of procrastination, television offers limitless opportunities for delay. With the number of available channels and shows, there's something for everybody. We don't recommend the news, however, as it may cause stress, anxiety, or, in rare cases, the desire to actually do something. Here are some excellent ways to expand your video procrastination repertoire:

- **Digital recorders:** You save the shows you like and watch them when you like. With a dual-tuner recorder, you can enjoy two shows at once, live, pausing one during the commercials and watching the other in the meantime!

- **Video games:** Talk about a time suck! With games for any interest, gender, and age, there's no reason to deny yourself.

- **Mailbox movies:** With companies like Netflix and Blockbuster, order movies online then watch the DVD magically appear in your mailbox. Be careful about ordering too many at once, though, because you may have to procrastinate on viewing them, turning them into work.

Reading

If you're a bookworm procrastinator, you know how many hours can pass with a good book. Select an author who's written many titles in a series so that you can move easily from one to the next. For maximum procrastination yield, don't try to read anything too intellectual. Reading only counts as BS if it's for school or work; anything else is BBTV.

Cooking

We've got to eat, so cooking falls under BS. If you opt to go in the gourmet direction, cooking can take up far more time than you might think. Start with grocery shopping, patronizing multiple stores to find just the right ingredients. Then spend the rest of the afternoon or evening chopping and simmering.

Sleep

Sleep straddles the BS-BBTV divide. On the one hand, it's a total escape, especially naps. On the other, it's necessary for one's health, and few of us get enough of it (see chapter 1,

"Introduction: Expand Time with Procrastination").

Again, right on the BS-BBTV line. It's important to show Fido and Fluffy the love, but doting on your adopted mammal is also a great way to pass some serious time. If you have a dog, hit the yard or dog park. With a cat, curling up on the couch is a good way to go, or break out the string and feathers.

In the Office

While there aren't as many diversionary activities in the office as in the home, and, as noted in chapter 6, it's necessary to maintain a certain degree of discretion when nonperforming on someone else's dime, there's still plenty of procrastinatory pleasure to be had at work.

The Internet

What the television is for the home, the Internet is for the office—and any day now, they're going to be one and the same. You can spend hours on the Internet participating in the following:

Procrastinators' Hall of Fame: St. Augustine

St. Augustine, one of the founding fathers of Western Christianity, didn't start off quite so holy. The man who later said "Lustful sex is the enemy of God" left the Christianity of his upbringing to live a hedonistic lifestyle, keeping a concubine for 15 years. Before he finally took his vow of chastity (at age 32) he had such a difficult time relinquishing the pleasures of the flesh that he prayed to God, "Give me chastity and continence, but not yet."

- **Games:** There are thousands of games online, from role-playing to chess to solitaire.

- **Celebrity news and gossip:** These sites are updated multiple times a day, so keep on checking!

- **Job searches:** Peruse what else is out there while you're still getting paid, and find out what everybody else is making in your position by performing a salary comparison search.

- **Shopping:** From cars to computers to chocolates, you can buy anything online. Auction sites such as eBay make shopping fun, while certain stores offer deep discounts on desirable items.

- **Dating:** Window-shop for potential new romances (but don't actually go out on a date, because that would be productive).

- **Working on better projects:** Got a big report due and all you want to do is learn to draw comics? Educate yourself—you may just find a new career!

Email and IM-ing

While you need to keep up with email at work, it's almost always less urgent than other projects, making it a top-notch form of BS procrastination. IM-ing and chatting with your friends is like being at the bar while you're still sitting at your desk, but BBTV all the way.

Gossip

If they didn't want you to do it, why would they have put in a water cooler?

Procrastivocabulary

Procrastiblog, Procrastichat, or **Procrastisurf:** Various modes of online procrastination.

Procrasticrap: To use the bathroom as a work-avoidance technique.

Procrastidate: Repeatedly rescheduled date or meeting.

Procrastifarian: One who smokes marijuana while procrastinating.

Procrastineat: To eat instead of doing whatever you're supposed to be doing.

Procrastishower: To take a long shower or bath in lieu of productive activities.

Procrastistalk: To track others, especially potential romantic partners, on Facebook or MySpace rather than working.

Procrasturbate: To pleasure oneself as a procrastination device.

Smoking

Yes, it's bad for you, but it affords lots of breaks and social time with the other pariahs.

Out in the World

If all you do is shuttle between office and home, you're not taking advantage of some prime procrastination activities. Try to step out in order to mix things up; otherwise, your standby procrastination pastimes will begin to seem stale.

Errands

An excellent BS technique, errands provide the perfect excuse to leave your chair and climb into the car. When you're feeling pressured, find an urgent need to buy stamps or drop off dry cleaning. Other popular errands include grocery shopping, beer runs, and ATM withdrawals.

Staying in Touch

One of the first things to suffer when you're not procrastinating is your social life. If you've got responsibilities to take care of, go out with old pals, rekindle a friendship, or visit your Grandma.

Partying

Killing two birds with one stone, when you party, you not only spend time with friends and meet new ones, you also drink away the desire to work.

Procrastination Is Your Oyster

We hope you've gotten some tempting ideas for activities to enjoy while you procrastinate. However, the only limit to what you should be doing when you're not doing what you're supposed to be doing is that it has to

Deferred Words

"Deep down, I'm enormously lazy. I like living, breathing better than working."
—Marcel Duchamp

be something you want to be doing. Let your heart be your guide as you determine your recreational choices and you won't go wrong. Now that you're a relatively advanced procrastinator, we'll take a look at some ways to cultivate your procrastination style, from keeping up the pace to surrounding yourself with pro-procrastination friends.

CHAPTER 8
AVOID THE PITFALLS: YOUR PROCRASTINATION STYLE

TO BECOME A PROCRASTINATOR IS one thing, but it's quite another to sustain it over the long haul and live among those who worship the gods of punctuality and productivity. Anybody can be a visitor to the land of procrastination; to be a resident requires commitment and dedication. While procrastination yields countless rewards, like any worthwhile pursuit, it also comes with challenges. In this chapter, we'll review some of the common pitfalls for the new procrastinator. We'll arm you with approaches for dealing with others who don't support your new lifestyle and help you identify fellow procrastinators so you can build a community of like-minded late-niks. You'll learn:

- How to climb back on the procrastination wagon.

- Whether you should inform authority figures (bosses, teachers, etc.) of your new philosophy.

- Which publications and television shows will sabotage your mindset.

- Why you should avoid libraries.

- How to spot another procrastinator at 20 paces.

Lapses and Slips

When you're enjoying your new way of life, it's hard to imagine sliding back into your former addiction to timeliness and responsibility. In your weaker moments, however, the old rhythms, the punctuality pushers, and the nattering naysayers will choose to strike, and even the most convicted among us will succumb to their pull. If you know their likeness and their tactics, you have a greater chance of successful resistance. You can retreat to higher moral ground among those who believe what you do, and your commitment to procrastination will be secure. Here's what you need to watch out for:

Falling Back into Old Habits

It's hard work becoming a new you. Sometimes the old ways resurface, and before you know it, you're toiling away on a project that isn't due for weeks. Remember that your former habits of efficiency and productivity were in place for years or decades. Until you've been a procrastinator for that long, you're at risk of backsliding. Combat this tendency with two approaches: one, sympathize with yourself for the inevitable slip; and two, hoist yourself right back onto the wagon when a slip occurs. It's all too easy to say "I messed up. I might as well keep messing up, as I've already ruined it." Instead, tell yourself "That was one slip. I recognized it, I've analyzed it, and I'm getting back on course."

Self-Doubt

You may sometimes doubt your new plan, wondering if you made the right choice with procrastination. In these moments, remember that any significant decision has pros and cons, and you have chosen the one for which the benefits significantly outweigh the downsides.

> ## Deferred Words
>
> "I love deadlines. I love the whooshing noise they make as they go by."
>
> —Douglas Adams

Tamp down your thoughts of doubt, grab the remote, and let the soothing glow of the television lull you into a relaxed mood. Or, pour a drink and call a pro-procrastination friend who will remind you of the advantages of procrastination and why you adopted it in the first place.

The Negative Influence of Others

You've worked so hard to get to where you are now; don't let judgment from efficient achievers derail your good work. Return to this book for comfort and reassurance and remember that people

attack that which they fear in themselves. You chose procrastination because
you are an independent thinker; if you
allow others to sabotage your ability to
think for yourself, you will let them win.

Naysayers and Efficiency Mongers

Not everyone encourages a life of leisure and
delay. With procrastination, you are on the
forefront of a formerly fringe movement that
grows by the day. Until procrastinators are
in the majority, however, you will encoun-
ter negative feedback. For some, this stems
from jealousy at the newfound freedom they
see you enjoying. Authority figures may take
your laidback attitude as an insult, and a
significant other will selfishly focus on how
your new attitude affects them. While you
haven't made a public proclamation that
you're now a procrastinator, soon enough

people will notice. Below is a list of people to watch out for, and some suggestions on how to handle them.

Bosses, Teachers, and Other Authority Figures

Because they expect you to handle a variety of tasks in a timely way, authority figures are most likely to discourage your new outlook. Rather than supporting you, they will continue to impose trumped-up deadlines, characterizing them as "drop dead" or "do or die." Don't fall for it. These are common scare tactics promulgated by those who don't understand procrastination. Vague reassurance is the best approach with authority figures. They need to feel confident that you'll get the job

Don't Set a Date

Octavio Guillen and Adriana Martinez of Mexico finally got married in June 1969, after a 67-year engagement. Both were 82 years old when they wed.

done, regardless of how and when. But don't pin yourself down to specific parameters of time or quality. Never lose your cool, as this will provide the sought-after chink in your procrastination armor. Always be even-keeled and kind, persuading them that you're on the job even when you're actually taking a mental break.

Naysayers

One common naysayer tactic is to call the procrastinator "lazy." When performed well, all worthwhile pursuits look easy from the outside, and procrastination is no different. These negative individuals won't understand how much work you've put into your procrastination, and they certainly don't see all its yields. Don't try to convince these people of your position and beliefs—they've already made up their minds. If they fail to keep your best interests at heart, extract the naysayers from your life. If they can't be avoided, smile and ignore them.

Critical Loved Ones

In personal relationships and especially between romantic partners, non-procrastinators will frequently worry that procrastination is a problem, not a solution. Your loved ones may view your actions as a personal affront to them, focusing on how your time-freeing behavior affects their lives. Respond to these individuals with sympathy, for they are ignorant. Laugh away their calls for efficiency, productivity, and punctuality, and invite them out for drinks.

Anti-Procrastination Propaganda

Surely you've noticed the countless publications bent on pulling procrastinators off their paths. Recognize that this is for-profit propaganda, designed to sell to people's productivity weaknesses, and avoid it whenever you can. Some particular publications to shun include *Real Simple*, *O Magazine*, *Fitness*, *Self*, *This Old House*, *Southern Living*, *Better Homes and Gardens*, and *Martha Stewart Living*. These magazines are geared toward self-improvement, DIY, home maintenance, and time management, all areas the procrastinator should eschew.

Avoiding the Achievers

Due to their negativity and ignorance, you want to steer clear of efficiency mavens and productivity promulgators whenever possible. This will be far easier if you avoid their natural habitats.

Libraries

Libraries are a common gathering spot for overachievers. Were you to enter a library, you'd notice them huddled over a book, often seated alone, casting withering glances at anyone who dares to speak. Those fools who still visit the library when the Internet delivers the world to your house, and Barnes & Noble is available in a pinch, are individuals to avoid.

The Front Row

Procrastinators rarely go to class, let alone commandeer a seat in the front. These spots are all but reserved for students who have finished their homework and are eager to answer questions, their hands permanently in the air. Procrastinators should always deposit themselves at the very back when they choose to attend.

Community Centers

Who has time to volunteer with so much good television to watch? Community centers crawl with achievers

Procrastination "Support"

If you're procrastinating with a bit of Internet wandering or looking for some potential new do-it-later friends, beware of efficiency wolves in procrastinators' clothing: procrastination support groups. These organizations aren't going to help you procrastinate or introduce you to other good-time Charlies. Instead, their mission is to *cure* you of your procrastination—as if procrastination were a problem or, worse, a disease. There's even Procrastinators Anonymous (whose shame-inducing motto is "Procrastination is the grave in which opportunity is buried").

According to one source, the topic has yielded 223,000 pages on Google alone, of which over 3,000 are clinics, programs, and support groups—fortunately, less than 2 percent of the total. Despite low numbers, these are powerful groups, recommending such anti-procrastination propaganda as books like *The Now Habit* and *Do It Now*. Especially in the early stages of your procrastination development, you'll want to steer clear of this mentality. As a procrastinator, you're ahead of the curve in terms of societal acceptance, but you've made the right choice. Be strong in your conviction, avoid the naysayers, and eventually the others will catch up.

who not only want success in their own lives, they seek to help others as well. If you choose to set foot in a community center, you will most likely be roped into volunteering for something.

Gyms

Gyms are the devil's breeding ground. Like rats in a cage, exercisers need endorphins to feel superior. The all-too-evident fact that they are not delaying their fitness clearly brands them as enemies of procrastination.

Vegetarian Restaurants

Any health-themed eatery is worth avoiding. Such establishments are generally patronized by the productive and the self-righteous. Also, the food often tastes like sawdust.

How to Identify a Fellow Procrastinator

As you move out into the world, especially when visiting the procrastination-friendly locations below, you'll want to train yourself to recognize a few characteristics that identify like-minded individuals. Do note, however, that some of these characteristics are also common in friendly people, not just procrastinators.

- **Looks open to a conversation with others:** Is the person sitting alone with only a magazine or a pulp novel, or even without any reading material? Does he often glance around, smiling at others? Does he chime into other strangers' conversations? Maybe he'd like to talk politics, books, or celebrities. Be careful, however, as he may just be looking for some action.

- **Drinking at an "inappropriate" hour:** If someone is drinking away a weekday afternoon, they might just be avoiding something. Strike up a chat to hear their story.

- **Appears happy and relaxed:** A laidback demeanor is a sure sign of someone with few cares in the world . . . a procrastinator!

- **Not in a hurry:** A leisurely amble implies that an individual does not subscribe to destination- and speed-oriented culture. Get in stride and say hello!

- **Unshowered:** Poor personal hygiene often indicates a lack of gainful employment.

Where to Find Fellow Procrastinators

By seeking out others who share your new-found passion for procrastination, you not only help secure your lifestyle change as permanent, you also might learn a thing or two! Most seasoned procrastinators have signature tricks and tips that make procrastination their own, and plenty are willing to share. Prepare to be entertained as well as encouraged—your comrades' victory stories cast the procrastinator as a hero! And you'll probably find partners for that last-minute jaunt to the beach, weekday matinee, or midday drink.

- **Bars:** Bars are primarily patronized by procrastinators, especially early in the day. Keep an eye open at the video games—especially video golf—for fellow delayers.

- **Head shops:** Procrastinators are often smokers and tokers.

- **Mini-marts:** Your brethren rarely manage to do a real grocery run, but often find themselves hankering for junk food late at night.

- **Movie theaters:** Though you likely won't *meet* other procrastinators at the movies, you can take solace in knowing the matinee is filled with others just like you.

- **Parks:** One of the happiest places for procrastinators, the park is filled with people enjoying a lovely day outside. Avoid the mothers and nannies, however; they view the park as a workplace.

- **Parties:** It's almost guaranteed that you'll find at least a few fellow procrastinators at parties. Relate anecdotes about tardiness and irresponsibility and see how they respond—if favorably, you've probably found a new friend.

- **Coffeehouses:** Despite the stimulant properties of coffee, cafés were invented for procrastinators. Smart proprietors have thus outfitted these establishments with wireless Internet, electrical outlets, and comfy chairs. Join your comrades for a jolt of espresso and think about writing a screenplay or a memoir (just *think* about it—don't actually *do* it). Maybe another procrastinating pal wants to bounce a few ideas off you, pick your brain, or merely use you to help her avoid her project. Sit back, relax, sip your caramel macchiato, and participate in the life of the mind.

- **Video rental stores:** Is someone picking up a lot of movies? They're probably

> ## Majority Rules
>
> Three out of four American college students consider themselves procrastinators.

avoiding something! It's easy to strike up a conversation with someone at a video store by commenting on a movie they've selected or asking if they have any recommendations. From there, you can see if they too are avoiding work. Soon enough you'll be passing the microwave popcorn.

It Takes a Village

By now you've cultivated myriad procrastination skills *and* learned how to find likeminded souls and shun naysayers. You're a procrastinator through and through, with the ability to avoid, delay, obfuscate, and lollygag. Unless you're independently wealthy, however, there are moments when you actually will need to get something done—but the procrastinator's way. In the next chapter, we'll explore how to know when it's time to work (at the last possible minute, of course) and how to complete necessities quickly and with the minimum possible effort.

VERY FEW PROCRASTINATORS ARE lucky enough to be able to avoid work entirely, to be freed from the onus of ever having to submit themselves to a task they don't want to perform. More than anything else in this book, the successful application of last-minute effort defines the expert procrastinator.

As a successful procrastinator, you will know when it's time to get started, pulling off that project or task you've spent countless hours avoiding. You will know how to harness the considerable power of the eleventh hour, drawing inspiration and motivation from the self-imposed time crunch.

Finally, you will have confidence in your ability to make it happen and contend with any contingency. As Henry Ford once said, "Whether you think you can or whether you think you can't, you're right!" So think you can! Sometimes you can't, however, and to that end we will equip you with tips about excuse delivery that will buy you more time *and* impress your friends in the retelling. Here's a sampling of what you'll learn:

- How to recognize the subtle hints of readiness.

- How the last minute can course like a drug through your veins.

- How to use miscommunication devices to delay delivery.

- How to positively spin failure.

Knowing When to Get Started

Experienced procrastinators point to a gut feeling that tells them when to start work. Until you cultivate that seventh sense in yourself, you'll want to look for a few common indicators that it's time for action:

You're Close to Not Having Enough Time to Finish.

Calculate how many hours you'll need to devote to a given project, divide this figure in half in order to motivate yourself and assure that you don't put in too much time, and determine how many hours you have left before the deadline. Be sure to calculate in sleep and food!

You're Thinking about the Project More than Before.

If you've tried to drink, distract yourself, or otherwise avoid thoughts about the project and nothing's working, it may be time to get started.

Someone Is Repeatedly Asking You about the Project's Progress.

Questions about progress generally imply the expectation that some work has been done. When the frequency of these inquiries accelerates and you're unable to stave them off, the time for work may be at hand.

There's an Emergency.

If your car breaks down, your child has lice, or the credit card is maxed out, it's probably time to buckle down and attend to the issues.

The Power of the Eleventh Hour

This is the moment you've waited for, the moment you've avoided as much as you've anticipated. The pressure is on—will you deliver? Of course you will! By harnessing the adrenaline that comes with waiting until the last minute, you'll be able to accomplish your task easily and quickly. Here are a few tips for making this exhilarating ride as smooth as possible:

- **Minimize interruptions.** Turn off the phone, quit out of email, and lock the door. Let friends and family know they shouldn't bother you.

Last-Minute Gains

The progenitor of the Parkinson's Law (see chapter 4, "Universal Procrastination Dynamics: Time Is a Human Invention"), C. Northcote Parkinson, explicated his theory thusly:

> General recognition of this fact is shown in the proverbial phrase "It is the busiest man who has time to spare." Thus, an elderly lady of leisure can spend the entire day in writing and dispatching a postcard to her niece. An hour will be spent finding the postcard, another in hunting for spectacles, half an hour in a search for the address, an hour and a quarter in composition, and 20 minutes in deciding whether or not to take an umbrella when going to the pillar box in the next street. The total effort that would occupy a busy man for three minutes all told may in this fashion leave another person prostrate after a day of doubt, anxiety, and toil.

The procrastinator inverts this phrase into "It is the savviest procrastinator who has time to spare," because the procrastinator enjoys herself until the last possible three minutes, then sends the postcard.

- **Turn off the television.** While the television is a friend to procrastination, it's counterproductive when you're finally trying to get the work done.

- **Be comfortable.** Wear stretchy clothing, put your hair in a ponytail, make sure the heat or air-conditioning is set.

- **Create a war room.** Arrange your workspace with everything you need close at hand. Stock up on caffeinated beverages, snacks, and, if necessary, cigarettes.

- **Psych yourself up.** You can do it! You're a procrastinator! The moment is now! Go team!

Delay Tactics

Even the most experienced procrastinator will sometimes miscalculate the amount of time necessary to complete a project. In order to gain yourself additional leeway, try the following:

- **Practice miscommunication.** Thanks to the cell phone, the expectation is you'll always be reachable. But everyone has experienced a dropped signal or voicemail snafu, and both can be faked. Most people will understand when you just aren't able to get through to ask a question critical to project completion. This generally buys only hours, not days, however.

- **Request an extension.** Let a boss or teacher know that you've hit a snag or that you've gotten so interested in the material that you want to explore additional options.

- **Blame computers.** Fortunately, despite technological innovations, computers and

Internet connections do fail, providing viable excuses when your project isn't done. Let's say you have a project due by 3:00 PM. It's noon, and you haven't even started. At a few minutes before 3:00, call your boss and frantically ask, "Did you get it? Did you get the paper?" She'll answer no, likely asking why. You will reply that you emailed her the project just before your computer crashed, and you're worried that all is lost. Assure her that you'll get to the root of the problem and have it to her as soon as possible. Not only have you bought yourself time but you've probably solicited some pity. Way to go!

- **Get help.** A pending deadline is a great time to call on friends to help you finish your project. If necessary, play the pity card. For example, say "If you don't help

me do this, I'll never get it done, I'll fail!"
No good friend would let that happen!

Excuses for Missed Deadlines

So you blew the original deadline. Don't fret—it happens to all procrastinators, and even sometimes to non-procrastinators, though they're loath to admit it. Instead, take this opportunity to learn new and creative ways to offer up excuses and try original spins on old classics.

Excuse delivery is an art unto itself, with various techniques, practices, and styles. One key to effective excuse presentation is knowing your audience to determine what will work on them, both in terms of excuse acceptance and the avoidance of further questions. For example, if you're a woman talking to a man in a suit, blaming a delay

Drug of Choice

In the final hours, caffeine is the procrastinator's best friend. Don't like coffee or tea? No problem. Not only can caffeine be ingested in cola, chocolate, energy drinks, and that old standby, NoDoz, it's been added to mints, breath strips, a slow-delivery skin patch, and even sunflower seeds.

on your menstrual cycle is an effective way to end the conversation.

Another crucial element is to keep excuses within the realm of possibility. Try to avoid such far-fetched stories as alien abduction, paper-eating dogs, or burning buildings from which you saved several elderly women. Make sure your excuse is neither traceable nor confirmable. Also keep in mind that the person hearing the excuse may already know a few things about you, and thus may be able to evaluate whether you're offering up something that you would actually do.

Complexity and Specificity

Injecting your excuse with complexity and specificity provides believability, especially when relying on a well-known classic. Elements of detail not only add credibility, they can be directed toward inspiring pity and extending a deadline. Additionally, if they're entertaining enough, your audience may be impressed or distracted away from their anger.

Rather than merely saying "I was sick," for example, you'll want to add a simple, graphic detail, such as "I was so sick that I couldn't get off the toilet." Not only will this bit of color make your story appear viable, it will discourage further questions. In the technology arena, don't simply say "My computer crashed." Instead, let your taskmaster know that "My hard drive crashed again. Though the patch Apple released a year ago is supposed to correct this particular problem, it didn't, and now all my data is lost, including everything related to this project. The guys at the Apple store say it will take about a week for my replacement drive to arrive, so I'm stuck using the computers at the library until then." You've not only bought yourself more time to pull off the project, but you've also garnered some pity.

Email

Email provides enough potential excuses that it merits its own discussion. If you're called out for failing to respond to a note or perform an emailed assignment, you've got access to countless technological scapegoats:

- "Your email must have gone into my spam folder."

- "We've been having a lot of network problems lately."

- "I receive so much email that I must have overlooked it."

- "I might have accidentally deleted it when cleaning out my folders."

- "I'm not sure what happened. I've had several people tell me emails they've sent didn't go through. I'll have my IT guy look into it and let you know what happened."

Unless the deadline in question has already passed, the sender is likely to resend the "missing" note, putting you once again on the hook.

After You Finish, Go Back to Procrastinating

Congratulations, procrastinator—you got something done, and not a moment before you had to. Now you can reap your reward—returning to procrastination. In a procrastinator's life, the normal ratio of lots of work to a little bit of play is reversed. You play most of the time, and every once in a while you do something. The upside to occasional action is the journey back to lethargy. You've come full circle!

WE HATE TO END THIS EVOLUTION on a sour note, but unfortunately it's a vital lesson to your procrastination growth: what were you thinking when you came close to finishing this book? At the very least, we hope you delayed the entire read, putting the book down for months at a time, only picking it up again at the last possible second before productivity and efficiency threatened you to the brink of madness.

In chapters 5 and 8, we outlined the perils of the self-help movement and its dissemination of productivity propaganda. How do you expect to avoid that damaging message if you can't even apply it to your experience of this book? Yes, it's "Self-Hurt," but there's still a "self" in the series title. This book is about learning to do something and is therefore entirely optional. If it's optional and it's productive, you shouldn't be doing it.

But we're going to give you a chance to redeem yourself: put this book down and walk away. Don't read to the end, don't wait to find out what happens. Are you still reading? What's wrong with you? Have you learned nothing in the preceding pages?

On the other hand, you may not view this book as work. Perhaps you're procrastinating doing something else in order to edify yourself on procrastination, a successful student of the bait-and-switch modality. If such is the case, reading this book was an active choice, and procrastination is about nothing more than the freedom to make your own decisions. Indeed it is the dictatorial rigors of our rushed, deadline-driven society that make *How to Procrastinate* necessary. When most people spend their time marching to someone else's drum, we should celebrate when someone takes a stand and decides to procrastinate, even if in so doing that person actually finishes a book.

So you see, yet again we have come full circle in the procrastinatory hall of mirrors. To finish the book implies non-procrastination, but in order to become a procrastinator you must finish this book. This is precisely the sort of conundrum you should ponder late at night with friends, fueled by the substances of nonproductivity.

As you participate in the world as a procrastinator, be sure to spread the word to those you suspect may be in need of procrastination's many benefits. You'll want to be careful not to proselytize to those who aren't yet ready to hear the message, avoiding the mistakes of religious missionaries who travel door-to-door with no regard for whether residents want to hear their message. When you see the signs of overwork and frustration in another good soul, however, gently test the waters. Upon encouragement, describe the joy of procrastination and welcome a new procrastinator into the world.

Or do it "tomorrow."